Author biography

Writer is an avid scholar of international relations and geopolitics.He has written various books on different subjects.

CONTENTS

Battlefield Ukraine-Putin's Spanish Laboratory!

Weapons and tactics re-testing for another world war?

Dr. Jack P. Andreu

ISBN 978-93-5610-396-2
© Dr. Jack P. Andreu 2022
Published in India 2022 by Pencil

A brand of
One Point Six Technologies Pvt. Ltd.
123, Building J2, Shram Seva Premises,
Wadala Truck Terminal, Wadala (E)
Mumbai 400037, Maharashtra, INDIA
E connect@thepencilapp.com
W www.thepencilapp.com

DISCLAIMER: *The opinions expressed in this book are those of the authors and do not purport to reflect the views of the Publisher.*

Ukraine-the nature's heaven

Before opening of war, Ukraine was a serene, peace loving and beautiful country full of natural beauty which attracted millions of tourists every year throughout the world, now it is almost shattered to pieces.

Operation Ukraine-Some Developments

The Russian forces are stationed in different places as in the previous days. Although they have not launched a new offensive, military sources say they are now preparing to take full control of southern Ukraine. Their main target is Odessa. Occupying this area, the whole area from Kherson through the Moldova border to Transnistria will come under Russian control. Meanwhile, a ceasefire has been declared again to evacuate civilians from the besieged Mariapole. Ukraine's top security official said yesterday that Russia's war command had turned its attention to the southern front to isolate the country from the Black Sea. Kiev, Kharkiv, Mariapol, Mykolaiv, Chernihiv and Odessa are strategically important, and Russian troops plan to encircle the cities and block the movement of Ukrainian troops. In this regard, the President of Ukraine Zelensky said that the Russian forces have targeted Odessa for a terrible bomb attack. At the same time, Russian President Vladimir Putin has sternly warned the West that Russian forces will only stop fighting if Russia's security is ensured. Russian Defense Ministry spokesman Igor Konashenkov said his country's troops had shot down four Ukrainian Sukhoi-27 fighter jets in the past 24 hours. Russian forces have defused Ukraine's Starkostiyantiniv air base with long-range high-precision missiles. At the same time, a 24-hour Ukrainian-controlled S-300 missile defense system was destroyed and 10 planes and helicopters were shot down. In retaliation, Ukraine's Defense Ministry said Russia had lost eight planes and helicopters since the start of the war. A number of Russian pilots have also been detained. Several Russian equipments were seized in the Mykolyav region. The Defense Ministry says more than 11,000 Russian troops have been killed by Ukrainian forces so far. However, the ministry did not say how many Ukrainian soldiers were killed in the fighting. Ceasefire declared again in Mariapole: A new ceasefire was declared yesterday in the Ukrainian city of Mariapole. The ceasefire should be effective from 10 am to 6 pm local time (2 pm to 1 pm Bangladesh time). Civilians will have the opportunity to leave the city at this time, the announcement said. However, it was not known how effective the ceasefire was. It is to be noted that a humanitarian corridor was launched to evacuate the people by declaring a ceasefire the day before. But Russia claims that Ukrainian troops did not allow any people to leave the city. They were threatened with being shot. In addition, pro-Ukrainian guerrillas blew up a building and violated the ceasefire. Russia alleges they are being held to use civilians as human shields. On the other hand, the Ukrainian army claimed that the Russian army did not observe the ceasefire. They have continued firing. Observers say the Russian military is urging civilians to evacuate in order to prevent further casualties. As soon as they move away, a big attack will be launched. On the other hand, the Ukrainian army is not allowing civilians to leave to prevent this attack. Earlier on Saturday night, Russian Defense Ministry spokesman Igor Konashenkov said that in violation of the declared ceasefire, Ukrainian extremist nationalists continued to attack Russian troops and Kiev failed to stop them. Due to this, the Russian army started the operation again from 6 pm on Saturday. Russia has declared a ceasefire in order to prevent civilian casualties during the Russian offensive. Moscow said the ceasefire should be used to evacuate civilians from the two cities so that civilian casualties would not be taken into account in future operations. But Russian news agencies say Ukraine's military is blocking the exit of civilians through the country's declared safe corridor. Putin says Western sanctions are tantamount to declaring war: Russian President Vladimir Putin has said that "the sanctions imposed on Russia by the Western world after the invasion of Ukraine are tantamount to declaring war." But thank God that time has not come yet. ' Putin warned that any attempt to create a "no-fly zone" over Ukraine would be seen as part of an armed conflict. He noted that he wanted to protect the Russian-speaking community in Ukraine on the basis of justice. "Our military will do everything possible," he said, referring to "Western defense analysts' allegations that the Russian military operation is less than expected." Russia's armed forces have almost completed the destruction of Ukraine's military infrastructure. This special military operation is going according to plan. ' Zelensky calls on people to go to war He called on the people of Ukraine, including Kiev, to go to war to defend the country. "We have to fight against the enemies," he said. So you have to get out of your house and drive the enemies out of our cities. '"

Russia claims Zelensky has fled to Poland. Earlier on Friday, Ukrainian opposition lawmaker Ilya Kiva told the media that President Zelensky had fled the country and was staying at the US embassy in Warsaw. In other news, an elite commando force consisting of 150 US Navy SEALs and more than 60 British Special Air Service commandos is stationed at a base in Lithuania to take Zelensky elsewhere. Russia, Ukraine to hold third round of talks Russia, Ukraine to hold third round of talks on Monday However, the details of where this meeting is taking place have not been disclosed. The first meeting between the two countries took place on the Ukraine-Belarus border. Although he did not provide details about the third round of talks, Ukrainian negotiator David Arakhamia confirmed the matter in a Facebook post, saying that Russia had only said that the meeting could take place on Monday. Israeli Prime Minister Naftali

Bennett has embarked on a diplomatic initiative to end the war with Ukraine. He arrived in Moscow yesterday and held a three-hour meeting with Russian President Vladimir Putin at the Kremlin. After the meeting, he spoke on the phone with Ukrainian President Volodymyr Zelensky. An Israeli official said Prime Minister Bennett was in talks with the United States, France and Germany to mediate the Ukraine war. A spokesman for Bennett said the Israeli prime minister had left for Berlin after meeting with Putin. There he will hold talks with German Chancellor Olaf Schultz. Meanwhile, French President Emmanuel Macron spoke with Israeli Prime Minister Naftali Bennett Putin before leaving for Moscow for a meeting, according to the Elysee Palace, the French president's residence. He briefed Bennett on what Macron had said to Putin. An Elysee Palace official said: "There will be close contacts between them to ensure a ceasefire in Ukraine. The German Chancellor will also be present. According to the report, Israel has offered to mediate in the military conflict between Ukraine and Russia on behalf of Ukrainian President Zelensky. The Prime Minister of Israel has taken the role of mediator in this case. However, officials believe that there will be no success in ending the war in Ukraine through the mediation of Bennett. Israel, known as a close ally of the United States, has condemned Russia's military intervention in Ukraine. Expressing solidarity with Kiev, it is also sending humanitarian aid to Ukraine. However, Israel said its government would maintain close contact with Moscow in order to resolve the conflict in Ukraine.

Hitler's Spanish Laboratory

When the Spanish Civil War broke out, Hitler and Mussolini provided military support to the rebels led by General Francisco Fanko. Russia then provided assistance to the government side. About 30,000 volunteers fought the rebels called the International Brigade. In this war, Germany and the Soviet Union simultaneously tested their advanced technology weapons. In 1939, the rebels led by Fanko won the civil war. Although Franco played a neutral role during World War II, he supported the Axis Powers. They later sent volunteers for Germany on the Eastern Frontier. German involvement began a few days after the war began in July 1936. Adolf Hitler quickly sent strong air and armored units to help the nationalists. The war provided combat experience for the German army with the latest technology. However, this intervention risked the escalation of World War II for which Hitler was not prepared. He therefore limited his support and instead encouraged Benito Mussolini to send large Italian units. The Multitasking Condor Legion was formed in Nazi Germany, a unit consisting of Luftwaffe and German Army (Hier) volunteers from July 1939 to March 1939. The Condor Legion proved particularly effective during the 1938 Battle of Toledo. Germany moved African troops to mainland Spain in the early stages of the war. German campaigns gradually expanded to include strike targets, notably - and controversially - the Guernsey bombings, which killed 200 to 300 civilians on April 2, 1936. Germany also used the war to test new weapons, such as the Lufthansa Junker Jun 8 Stuka and Junkers 22 June transport trimotors (also used as bombers), which proved effective. German involvement was further highlighted by the launch of Operation Ursula, a U-boat-like initiative;

And the contribution of Craigsmarin. The team achieved many nationalist victories, especially in air warfare, when Spain provided a field of evidence of further German tank tactics. The training given by the German units to the nationalist forces will prove invaluable. At the end of the war, perhaps 56,600,000 nationalist soldiers, infantry, artillery, aircraft and navy were trained by the German separatists. About 1,000 Germans were killed in the war, and about 300 died, although no more than 10,000 took part. At the cost of 1939, German aid to the nationalists amounted to about 5 215,000,000, of which 15.5% was used for salaries and expenses and 21.9% for direct supplies to Spain, while 622.6% was spent on the Condor Army. In all, Germany provided the nationalists with 600 planes and 200 tanks.

There are many similarities between Putin and Hitler. Hitler craved for the estranged lands of Germany in the second world war. Likewise Putin also craves for the estranged lands of former Soviet. Before the starting of world war 2, Hitler annexed some lands of other europen countries. In 2014, Putin invaded and annexed Crimea, likewise is it not that Ukraine battle field is becoming more and more a testing ground for testing Russian and NATO war tactics and weapons?

The Doomsday Plane

Russia is one step ahead, America can not step forward? Russian President Vladimir Putin has ordered the country's nuclear arsenal to be ready within a week of the Ukraine attack. Soon after, the United States completed its first test flight of a nuclear-armed aircraft. As if indirectly convincing Moscow that America is ready for a possible nuclear war! The test flight of the nuclear-armed anti-nuclear aircraft took place on February 26 in the Midwestern US state of Nebraska. The Pentagon says the US Air Force's nuclear-armed anti-aircraft gun was flown experimentally from an air base in Nebraska on Monday. The plane was flown to Chicago in a four-and-a-half-hour flight. Several jets were flown before the plane took off. To keep an eye on the ballistic missile so that it does not hit the plane suddenly. According to experts, the Boeing-747 model aircraft has been built with nuclear weapons. Whose name is 'Boeing-E4B'. It also has a nickname. 'Last Day Plane (Doomsday Plane)'. The Pentagon says the nuclear-armed aircraft was part of the US Air Force's nightwatch fleet of the 1970s. The United States built the aircraft in order to maintain communication between the top echelons of the various branches of the military during the nuclear war and to convey their instructions without hindrance. Experts say the 200 million aircraft did not have a digital system. The communication system of the pre-digital era has been used. So that the aircraft does not become immobile, inactive, in the electromagnetic waves of intense strong frequencies created by the impact of an atomic bomb or an atomic explosion. The plane has no windows. Apart from the pilot and assistant driver, passengers can also be on this plane. The aircraft has three layers of protective coating outside the aircraft to prevent it from igniting due to the tremendous amount of heat generated by the atomic bomb. The aircraft has more than 75 satellite dishes and antennas in different parts of its head. So that the aircraft can communicate instantly from the sky to ships, submarines, passengers and warplanes and all landline telephones in any part of the world.

Dangerous combat drone Bayrektar TB-2

Ukraine is using Turkey's dangerous war drone Bayrektar TB-2 in the war against Russia. With this drone, Ukraine blew up a train loaded with Russian oil. This train was going to supply fuel to the Russian army. Not only did the Ukrainian media claim that the drone system had destroyed an entire Russian military column near Kharkiv, but the question was how much support could this dangerous fighter drone have for Ukraine in the face of Russia? Let us know how this Turkish drone came to be discussed and what its significance is for Ukraine.

Bayrektar- This name now creates fear in the army. The sound of this drone flying in the sky spread panic as soon as it reached the enemy forces below. The soldiers dropped their belongings and started running. Proven power in the Armenia-Azerbaijan war During the Nagorno-Karabakh war between Armenia and Azerbaijan last year, the Turkish-made fighter drone scattered the Armenian army like a packet of cards. The Armenian army, which had been occupying Karabakh for three decades, was defeated and re-occupied by Azerbaijan. Now these drones are wreaking havoc in the Russian-

Ukrainian war. The Ukrainian military has also released footage of its use. Reports from the battlefield also suggest that Ukraine is using Bayrektar TB-2. A statement from Ukraine's military said on Saturday that the bomber struck shortly after noon in front of a Russian military base. It was going to supply fuel for the Russian army. According to Ukrainian media reports, the drones have wreaked havoc on the Russian military near Kharkiv. It destroyed an entire column of the Russian army. There have been many videos on social media praising Ukrainian troops, but during last year's war, Azerbaijani military forces began releasing footage of drone strikes, causing fear among the Armenian army. Ukraine started buying these drones from Turkey in 2019. Ukraine has also acknowledged that it is using drones against Russian forces. At the same time, citing the military, Russian news agencies have demanded that a number of TB-2 drones be shot down. The state news service Sputnik has made similar demands. However, most tweets with such claims have now been deleted. This drone is very powerful The unmanned drone TB-2 can fly at 138 miles per hour (222 kilometers per hour) and carry four smart missiles, or 330 pounds of explosives, according to the Turkish defense company Baker, which makes the barricade. The drone is 39 feet long and 21 feet wide and can fly up to 18,000 feet. This drone has been used in war and it has proved its capability. Although it proved to be very effective during the Armenian war, its flaws were also exposed. The Turkish military is using them in Syria. Kurdish forces have also become their target. This drone has proven to be quite effective in destroying ground-powered tanks and air defense systems. Another special feature of this drone is that it can evade the air defense system. But the situation in Russia is different The Russian army has far more advanced and advanced military technology than Armenia. In this context, the question arises whether this drone can prove to be equally effective against Russia? Mark Kansian, a senior adviser at the Center for Strategic and International Relations Studies, said in a recent article that the war between Russia and Ukraine would test the capability of tanks on the ground today. After the Battle of Karabakh, defense analysts raised serious questions about the capabilities of the tanks. The Turkish-made Birector drone scattered Armenian tanks like packets of cards and proved ineffective. Can these drones stop Russia? Russia has about 2,840 tanks, and Russia is deploying them in large numbers in Ukraine. Now the question is whether the bioreactors will be able to stop these tanks from advancing. Russia's military analysts claim that the boycott will not be very effective in front of Russia because the Russian military has advanced radar systems that can warn in advance of their occurrence in the sky. Another strong point of the Russian military is its cyber capabilities. If Russia stops the boycott on the basis of a cyber attack, it could prove to be a turning point. Military analysts believe that Russia has studied the effects of barricade drones during the wars in Syria and Karabakh and has developed a strategy against them. "TB-2 was very successful in the Azerbaijan-Armenian war,

Ukraine has launched a drone strike to disperse a Russian military convoy. And the sophisticated and lethal drone called BERACTOR TB-2 is playing an important role in this attack. Enemy convoys are being targeted with these drones. Using these drones against Armenia in November 2020, Azerbaijan destroyed their military. This drone brought great success in that war. But this time the opponent is Russia. Whose huge military power. Sophisticated armament. As a result, the perspective is also very different. It is true that the Russian convoy is being attacked by these drones, but at the same time the question is whether this drone, which has brought success against

Armenia alone, will be able to hold its own against Russia? However, Ukraine is relying on these drones. What could be the effect of Russia dropping 100 kiloton atomic bomb on Kiev? This Turkish-made Barractor drone is one-eighth the weight of the American MQ-9 Ripper drone. Capable of hitting targets at 128 km per hour, the drone can carry four MAM laser-guided missiles. And much more perfect in terms of attack. This drone is capable of flying for 28 hours. Its communication range is 296 km. This drone can fly at an altitude of 25,000 feet. It can hit a target at a distance of 6,000 kilometers. Chief of the Ukrainian Air Force Lieutenant General Mykola Oleschuk called the drone a "life saver." Ukraine bought the drone from Turkey in 2019. Apart from Armenia, the drones have had great success in Libya, Syria and the Nagorno-Karabakh conflict.

Czech Hedgehog

A group of young men in the city of Lviv, the largest city in western Ukraine, are building a 'check hedgehog' at home with an iron bar that has been used to stop the Russian army. This 'Czech Hedgehog', made of a large sheet of iron, was used on the border between Czechoslovakia (now the Czech Republic) and Germany during World War II to intercept opposition tanks. The structure was built to block the path of the opposition army. Thirty young people from Lviv are making it by watching tutorials on the internet. Taras Philipchak formed an alliance of friends shortly after Russia's military operation in Ukraine began last week. He also shared his plans on Facebook and Twitter and requested to be involved in this work. "The brother came and said, 'We have to stop the Russian tanks anyway.' That's when the idea came to my mind. " Philip Chuck was involved in the construction of a house in Lviv. From there, he collected discarded iron and started making 'Check Hedgehog' with his friends. They have already made several. Each structure weighs about 100 kilograms. Filippchak said he was planning to send the structure to the whole of Ukraine so that Ukrainian troops could use it.

Ukraine's Javelins Overpowers Russ Grad

After a week of bombings and long-range 3-M54 caliber cruise missiles, Russian forces are now fighting for control of several Ukrainian cities, including Kharkiv. But in that operation, they are facing stiff resistance from the Ukrainian army, occupying virtually every inch of land. However, on Thursday, the eighth day of the war, Russian forces captured the port city of Kherson, at the mouth of the Danipar River in southern Ukraine. Attacks have also been stepped up to capture Odessa and Mariupol, two major cities on the Black Sea coast. One week ago, the

Russian navy, deployed along the Crimean coast snatched from Ukraine in 2014, began operations to capture the two cities. Thousands of troops landed on the Russian Navy's Amphibian Landing Vehicle and took up positions around Odessa and Mariupol. After Russian President Vladimir Putin announced a military operation against Ukraine on February 24, Moscow launched air strikes as well as long-range cruise missiles. The Russian Armored (equipped with tanks and armored vehicles) and artillery divisions then launched operations with Belarus, Donbass (Donetsk and Luhansk regions of Ukraine are collectively called by this name). Initially, Russian forces used 550-kilometer Toss-1 missiles to strike cities from a distance. The destructive power of this 'Multiple Launch Rocket System' (MLRS) mounted on T-72 tanks is deadly. But it is not effective in face-to-face fighting on city streets. In this situation, Putin's forces are relying on BM-21Grad. Over the past two days, they have been fighting in several cities, including Kharkiv and Kherson, using 500m-20km models of the MLRS mounted on vehicles. Russian tanks are also taking the lead in protecting Grad-carrying vehicles. In this situation, the main tool of the Ukrainian army to stop the Russian fleet is the FGM-148 javelin made in America. A number of Russian tanks have been destroyed in the past few days by one of the world's best anti-tank missiles. Some military experts believe that the javelin played a role in the withdrawal of Russian troops from the capital, Kiev. This light missile can easily carry only one army. The anti-tank missiles have already proved effective in the civil wars in Syria and Libya. Despite Kherson's capture, major cities, including Kiev, Kharkiv, Odessa, Mariupol, and Chernihiv, are still under Ukrainian occupation, according to a statement from the British Ministry of Defense on Thursday. In the last 72 hours, however, the Russian military has stepped up its preparations to launch a final offensive in several cities, including Kiev, according to intelligence reports.

Molotov cocktails

A group of young people wake up in the basement of a three-story apartment in Kiev in the dark of night. Molotov cocktails are being made at wartime pace. Kiwi is not the only capital. This cocktail is circulating in the hands of people all over Ukraine. Ukrainians new weapons to stop the Russians! No! This is not a drink. Rather bottled flammable liquid. The mouth of the bottle is closed with a piece of cloth. If necessary, the enemy can be wounded by setting fire to that piece of cloth and throwing a burning bottle. Locals have destroyed several Russian tanks on the streets of Kiev with this weapon, a bit like a bottle-bomb. She is also awake at night in the basement of Kiev. A couple of weeks ago, he quit his job as a project manager in a private company. He was due to join his new job on Monday. But now the shadow of the enemy in Shire! So he left and joined the Molotov cocktail makers. He also wants to build resistance in the country from eight to eighty against the Russian army. "It's more important than a new job," Olga said. The country's defense ministry has called on civilians to resist Vladimir Putin's forces after the invasion of Ukraine on Thursday. Putin's forces are wary of any move, and the ministry's call is: "Prepare the enemy by making Molotov cocktails!" Not just Molotov cocktails. Ukraine's Defense Ministry pleads, "Cut down trees and block roads." Put nets on the door of the house. If you find out that Russian troops are hiding in the jungle, set the whole forest on fire. The tree will grow again on the bones of the enemy. " Ordinary Ukrainians have responded to the government's call. They are on the battlefield to protect themselves from Putin's forces. But in secret. In the last few hours since the invasion of Ukraine, ordinary Ukrainians have been searching for the process of making Molotov cocktails, according to the Washington Post. Everyone's question on Google: How to make Molotov cocktail at home? As of Saturday, Putin's forces had killed 198 Ukrainian national security guards, according to US media reports. Besides, 1,115 civilians including 33 children were also killed. But is it possible to build resistance to these domestic weapons against the Russian armed forces on the road? According to John Spencer, head of urban warfare studies at the Modern War Institute in New York, every little resistance on the battlefield can work together. "The strength of the military doesn't matter in urban areas," Spencer said. He said, "When a whole nation unites and obstructs the fighters and separates them from the logistics, it becomes a trap."

Why such a powerful vacuum bomb

Has Russia used a vacuum bomb in the war against Ukraine? Several human rights groups around the world, including Ukraine, made the allegations against Vladimir Putin's government on Monday. However, Moscow has not officially commented on the matter. Human rights groups say Russia's use of the vacuum bomb in the war with Ukraine is tantamount to war crimes. Because of the 1949 Geneva Conventions, the use of these bombs on the battlefield was prohibited. Ukraine claims on Monday that Putin's forces used cluster munitions on its soil, as well as prohibited weapons. "Russia is wreaking havoc on Ukrainian soil," Osama Makarova, Ukraine's ambassador to the United States, told reporters after a meeting with lawmakers at the White House on Monday. Today (Monday) they used a vacuum bomb, which was banned at the Geneva conference. " Russia may have used banned weapons, such as the vacuum bomb, as well as the cluster bomb, according to Amnesty International. They further claimed that the target of the Russian attack was civilians in Ukraine. According to Amnesty International, Putin's forces attacked a pre-school in northeastern Ukraine on Friday morning with cluster munitions. The attack killed at least three people, including a child who had taken refuge at the school.

Many human rights groups, including Amnesty and Human Rights Watch, have strongly condemned the use of prohibited weapons such as clusters and vacuum bombs in the war against Ukraine. "Such attacks amount to war crimes," said Amnesty International Secretary-General Agnes Kalamard. Russia has not issued an official statement on the attack. The bomber struck shortly after noon in front of a U.S. military base.However, US media outlet CNN claimed that a number of rocket launchers, such as TOS-1 and TOS-1A, had been spotted on the Ukrainian border. These rockets are used to launch vacuum bombs.The United States has denied the allegations in a statement issued Friday stating "Similar, baseless allegations concerning Russia's intelligence have been made more than once. However, Washington has agreed with human rights groups. According to White House Press Secretary Jane Sackie, "if this allegation (of using a vacuum bomb) is true, it is a war crime." The Russian embassy in Washington declined to comment.What's so significant about a vacuum bomb?

Why did war experts call it the most powerful non-nuclear weapon? According to war experts, the most powerful non-nuclear weapon is the vacuum bomb. Although it is not possible to use it in air or water, it is a deadly weapon in land war. It is capable of making the bodies of many people disappear at the same time. In addition, the explosion of a vacuum bomb lasts longer than a normal bomb. To many it is also known as a thermobaric weapon or aerosol bomb.How does a vacuum bomb work? Why does it last longer than other explosions? After launching the bomb with a launcher or rocket launcher, it begins to absorb oxygen from the air. As a result, it plays more waves in the air than other bombs. Fuel-air explosives (FAEs) are the most lethal of the thermobaric weapons or vacuum bombs. Ordinary explosives contain 25 percent fuel and 75 percent oxidizer in a mixture of fuel and oxidizer like black powder. However, thermobaric weapons or vacuum bombs are almost 100 percent fuel.Vacuum bombs are almost entirely fuel-intensive, so they cannot be used underwater or at high altitudes or in extreme weather. But, on the battlefield, it is deadly in places like tunnels or bunkers. This is because as soon as it comes in contact with oxygen after an attack in a closed place, it starts a wave like explosion. According to Human Rights Watch, a 1993 report by the US military's intelligence agency mentioned the potential for a vacuum bomb. The report said that the lethality of the vacuum bomb was different from that of other explosives. The pressure of the strong waves of the explosion made it deadly. Under that pressure, the lungs burst.The pressure of the strong waves of the explosion made it deadly. Under that pressure, the lungs burst. If the type of vacuum bomb attack is different then the result is also different. The bomber struck shortly after noon in front of a U.S. military base. The bomber struck shortly after noon in front of a U.S. military base. Vacuum bombs typically use fuels such as ethylene oxide and propylene oxide, which are highly toxic. As a result, the target of the attack was surrounded by a cloud of toxic combustion in the burning state. As a result, the people in this place have to breathe in the clouds of that toxic chemical. Which penetrates their bodies and causes wounds. Another US report claims that the vacuum bomb attack caused more wounds inside the body.The history of the war shows that the United States was accused of using vacuum bombs, such as the FAI, in the Vietnam War. This was claimed in a 2000 report by the international human rights organization Human Rights Watch. In addition to the United States, war experts from the former Soviet Union were also involved in the development of vacuum bombs. According to Human Rights Watch, the FAI weapon, created by Soviet scientists in 1969, was used in the attack on China.Human Rights Watch claims that scientists have made the vacuum bomb even more deadly since then. Russia also claims to have third-generation warheads at the moment. Not just vacuum bombs. Ukraine is also waging an "unequal" war against Russia over its nuclear program. Russia has the world's largest nuclear arsenal, according to the Stockholm International Peace Research Institute (SIPRI). Putin has 6,350 warheads in his arsenal. In second place is America (five and a half thousand). China (350) or France (290), but insignificant compared to Russia or America.

The Moving crematorium

Russia is 'vanishing' the bodies of dead soldiers! Putin forces in Ukraine with a furnace inside the truck.From the outside, it looks like five ordinary trucks. However, there is a furnace hidden inside the truck. Vladimir Putin's forces are "vanishing" Russian soldiers killed in the war against Ukraine into the furnace. Not a truck, but a moving crematorium! In addition to armored vehicles or weapons and ammunition, Putin's forces have entered Ukraine with a number of specially designed trucks. That is the claim made by several Western media outlets, including Britain and the United States.According to the reports published in the western media, in 2013, for the first time, a picture of that 'running crematorium' appeared on the net. Russia-Ukraine war has been circulating on the net since Thursday. According to some war experts, the Putin government is also discrediting the actual number of casualties in the war by inserting the bodies of Russian soldiers into the burning furnace. Allegedly, Putin's forces also burned the bodies of ordinary Ukrainian people.Since the start of the war against Ukraine, there has been a storm of criticism from outside as well as inside Russia. Many citizens of his country have protested against President Putin. This time, the mothers of many Russian soldiers have also become vocal after the media made a fuss over the picture of the 'running crematorium'. A committee of mothers of Russian fighters has claimed that their sons were tricked and taken to Ukraine. It was reported that they were being taken to the Ukrainian border for military exercises. However, after going there, they were dropped directly on the bloody battlefield.Andrei Kurochkin, the deputy chairman of the committee, which was formed in 1979, said: "We are receiving countless phone calls from mothers all over Russia. They are crying. They don't know if their sons are alive. " Kurochkin further claims that many Russian soldiers' mobile phones have been confiscated since they were taken to Ukraine. Even if they do not agree to go to the battlefield to fight, they are being physically abused.According to Kurochkin, "in the event of a war, professionals should be sent." This is not the case with boys who have just joined the army. "He claimed that many Russian soldiers had been taken prisoner. He also expressed the view that it will bring disaster. Britain has spoken out against the Putin government for re-publishing pictures of the "ongoing crematorium". "If I had been in the Russian army and knew that the generals had no confidence in me, I would have been very worried," said Ben Wallace, the country's defense minister.He added, "Even if the parents of that soldier were worried. Because sending a crematorium to the battlefield means trying to cover up the damage caused by the war. " The committee, made up of mothers of Russian fighters, is also considering legal action over the issue. They want to file a written complaint with Russia's chief military prosecutor.Putin has refused to give up, despite protests against the war inside Russia. Official sources say he plans to surround Ukrainian forces in the capital, Kiev. So the Ukrainian forces surrendered within a week of the war.

Fight- the Stalingrad way

Some say 'Welcome to the gates of hell'. Somewhere or 'go to hell'. The Ukrainian army and the general public have written similar "messages" on both sides of the road leading to Kiev for the invading Russian forces. In addition, new "directions" have been set up overnight to confuse the Russian military. After Russian President Vladimir Putin declared war on February 24, Volodymyr Ariyev, a member of the Ukrainian parliament, said, "Our country and its people are ready to do anything to defend themselves." Preparations are under way to make Moltov cocktail bombs in every house in the capital Kiev. Apart from this, various steps are being taken to destroy the morale of the enemy. Examples are new roadside 'guides'. "We are doing everything we can to push the Russian army into the streets of hell," Ariyev said on Monday. Weapons have also been handed over to them. Vladimir Putin's army has not had much success fighting Ukraine since Sunday, despite striking progress in the first three days of the war. They have been waiting on the outskirts of Kiev for the last 48 hours. Because, there is a possibility of strong resistance when entering the city. Kharkiv, Ukraine's second-largest city, was captured on Friday, but lost control on Sunday in a counter-attack by Ukrainian troops and resistance forces. During the Second World War, the besieged Russian army and the general public fought against Hitler's forces in Stalingrad (now Volgograd) for five consecutive months. The German Nazis suffered their first defeat in that war. At that time, the Russian army used to write various messages on the walls to break the morale of the German forces. In the style of Stalingrad, this time Ukraine is trying to stop the Russian forces in the cities.

Chinese strategy to stop the advance of the Russian army

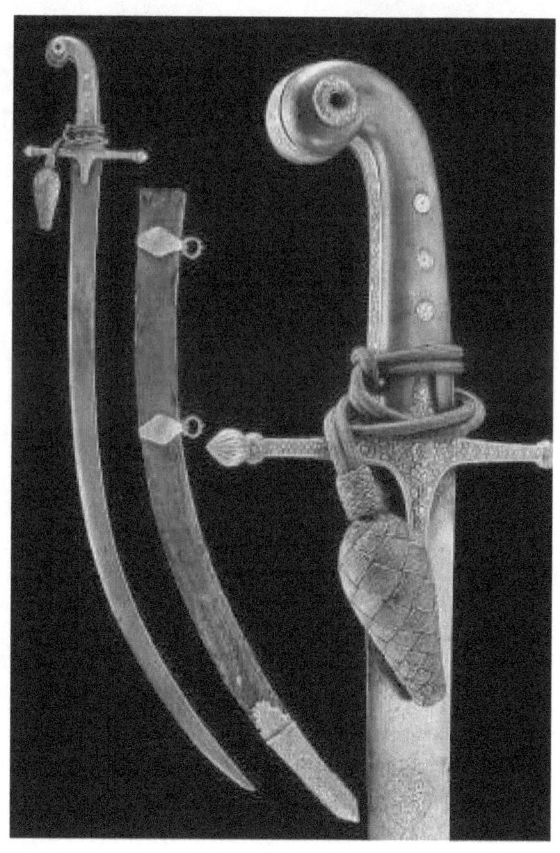

Ukraine's two-and-a-half-thousand-year-old Chinese strategy to stop the advance of the Russian army That policy was first applied by the Russian army during Napoleon's invasion of Russia. Stalin also fought against Hitler during World War II. In the 5th century BC, Chinese military expert Sun Zhu wrote in his Art of War about the tactics used in the fight against formidable opponents. During Napoleon's invasion of Russia in 182, Tsar (Russian Emperor) Alexander I's army was the first to apply the same policy. During World War II, Soviet President Joseph Stalin adopted a similar strategy to prevent the invasion of Hitler's forces. This time, the Ukrainian army has adopted the "scorched earth" war tactics to prevent the three-pronged attack of the Russian forces. The key to the 'scorched earth policy' is to slow down the progress of the powerful enemy army. Destroying roads, bridges, potential habitats and sources of juice during retreat is one of its components. The objective is one and the same, as the speed of the enemy's aggression slows down after repeated obstacles, there is time to build the next level of resistance. The morale of the invading forces is also likely to be affected. On the second and third days of the war, the army of Ukrainian President Volodymyr Zelensky followed suit. In the first day of fighting on Thursday, Russian forces took control of Kharkiv, the second largest city in Ukraine, and the Chernobyl nuclear power plant. After the capture of Kharkiv by Russian troops infiltrating the border between Donetsk and Luhansk (these two regions of eastern Ukraine are collectively called Donbass) declared by Russian President Vladimir Putin, they marched towards Kiev. On the other hand, the Russian tank brigade, which had crossed the Belarusian border in the north, proceeded with the same objective after capturing Chernobyl late on Thursday night. Troops crossing the Daniper River have already reached near the capital Kiev, crossing the Belarusian border. The third center of Russian aggression is the Crimean peninsula, which was snatched from Ukraine in 2014. A large number of Russian warships have already been deployed in the Black Sea. At the same time, the "Amphibian Landing Vehicle" was intended to quickly land troops on the mainland of Ukraine in the event of a war. With their help, Russian forces landed in Mariupol and Odessa, off the coast of southern Ukraine. The purpose of the Russian forces advancing from the south was to reach Kiev via the province of Kherson. In the face of a three-pronged attack, the Ukrainian army began destroying Kiev-bound bridges and roads one after another on various fronts since Thursday. While retreating, they are destroying their own army camps. Vitaly Skakun Volodimirovich, a battalion engineer of the Ukrainian navy, even stopped a Russian armored platoon by blowing up the Henichesk bridge by planting a mine on his body in Kherson. Russia won the war on self-defense against the "scorched earth policy" against Napoleon and Hitler's forces. It remains to be seen how they will deal with the 2,500-year-old Chinese strategy as invaders in Ukraine.